NORTHAMPTONSHIRE
PRIVIES

by

JULIE WILSON

COUNTRYSIDE BOOKS

NEWBURY · BERKSHIRE

First published 1997
© Julie Wilson 1997

COUNTRYSIDE BOOKS
3 Catherine Road
Newbury, Berkshire

ISBN 1 85306 475 0

Produced through MRM Associates Ltd., Reading
Typeset by Techniset Typesetters, Newton-le-Willows
Printed by Woolnough Bookbinding Ltd., Irthlingborough

CONTENTS

FOREWORD 5

1 THE GOOD OLD DAYS? 7

2 TYPES OF PRIVY 25

3 STORIES FROM AROUND NORTHAMPTONSHIRE 38

4 PARTICULAR PRIVIES 46

5 WHEN NEWSPAPERS WERE NOT JUST FOR READING 55

6 REVOLTING RODENTS AND OTHER HORRORS 59

7 A GOOD SHOVELFUL 65

8 POTTY PONTIFICATIONS 74

9 PUBLIC INCONVENIENCES 77

10 POSH LOOS 83

11 SERVICEMEN'S TALES 89

12 BURIED BUT NOT FORGOTTEN 92

A PRIVY BY ANY OTHER NAME 94

I am indebted to everyone who allowed me to photograph their privies, and to the many people who were happy to share their memories with me.

FOREWORD

At the grand old age of 94, my grandfather Fred Brice still uses his outside lavatory, and resists all talk of installing a more comfortable new indoor WC. Come hail or shine he ventures down the garden path to sit in a damp and chilly brick-built outhouse, but says it's all good exercise and a chance to get a bit of fresh air. As a young child I remember staying at his house and having to leave the warm, cosy fireside on freezing dark evenings and running back and forth to the loo as quickly as I could in fear of shadows, strange noises and the bogeyman.

It is unusual for anyone still to use outdoor lavatories, but it wasn't so long ago that virtually everyone had to make the most of some very primitive sanitary provisions – a great many people in Northamptonshire remember privies, which were commonplace in local towns and villages up to the 1930s and in some cases, even more recently.

In the course of researching this book I have been startled by the number of people with an interest in this rather unusual subject, and I am very grateful to all those who responded to my appeals for help in local newspapers.

I have found that many people with memories of using privies have been pleased that this small aspect of social history is being recorded, as it gives a good snapshot of life in the not too distant past and helps us to appreciate what we have today.

JULIE WILSON

The author in her role as Privy Inspector!

[1]

THE GOOD OLD DAYS?

It's so easy to take for granted our home comforts, with our warm, indoor flush lavatories and soft toilet paper. Yet it was not so very long ago that people had to suffer the most primitive sanitary conditions, with the abundance of raw sewage not only being unpleasant but also leading to horrific health problems. In Towcester, for example, 200 people died in the 1840s from an outbreak of cholera which was caused by the unhygienic conditions and dreadful overcrowding. It took a disaster on this scale to bring about the laying of new drains and the demolishing of the worst housing in Queens Street and Pomfret Road.

It was not until Victorian times that Northamptonshire saw anything vaguely resembling a modern lavatory, yet other civilisations had given great thought to the disposal of human waste many centuries before. Way back in 2000 BC the Minoans in Crete enjoyed flowing water, wooden seats and earthenware pans. When the Romans landed in Britain in 55 BC they must have been appalled by our total lack of sanitary provision, particularly as they had been used to luxurious public latrines and baths complete with flowing water, sewerage systems and filtered drinking water. Despite their good example, it took a long time before the locals started to clean up their act, and waste continued to flow into streams and rivers. However, there is evidence that a few of the county's nobler residents built garderobes or privies on their premises, albeit in a very basic way.

When Dr J. Alexander directed excavations at the site of Northampton Castle during four summers in the 1960s, archaeologists found evidence of a privy or garderobe room in the royal chambers, which dated back to the middle of the 12th

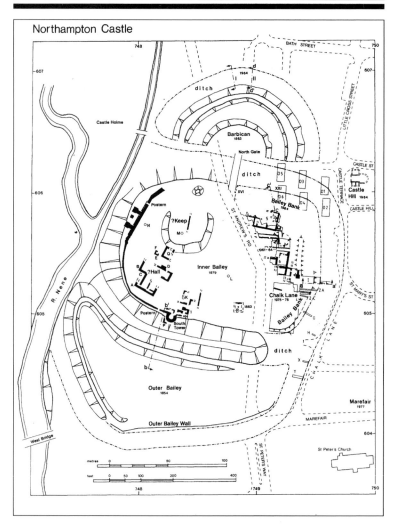

A plan of the castle showing Room B where the long-drop privy was located. (Northamptonshire County Council Archaeology Dept.)

8

Remains of Northampton Castle pictured in 1870. A long-drop privy was located in the royal chambers and sewage would fall from a hole on the first floor to a pit beneath, outside.

century. It appears that this was a 'long-drop' privy, in which the seat and hole would have been located in a first floor room which jutted out, enabling the sewage to trickle down the outside of the building into a large stone-lined pit outside. By examining the contents of this and other garderobe pits at the castle, the archaeologists were able to determine what these old Northamptonians ate. Not surprisingly, their food was fit for kings, and there is evidence that steaks, mutton, lamb, pigs' trotters, goose and duck were all on the menu. There were also bones from deer, hare, swans, heron and woodcock. Incidentally, the royal chambers were situated on the site of the little garden at the top of Chalk Hill car park.

9

Inside the former privy area of the guards' tower at Rockingham Castle.

It is hard to imagine how horrible it must have been for those at Northampton Castle and at other castles such as Rockingham near Corby. They had to put up with the smells and sight of raw sewage piling up against the building where long-drop privies were used, particularly in the heat of the summer. However, Towcester historian Brian Giddings says that these privies, which continued in use until the 17th century, were practical: 'The soil accumulated in the pit until it was collected and it was not covered so that bacteria could get to it. If it was buried it would stagnate and cause more problems, particularly if it was near to the water supply, which could have become affected.'

Long-drop privies have also been found at Barnwell Castle, to the north of the county, which was built in 1266. Here whole turrets have been devoted to privies on two floors, connected by a shaft to a pit, so that guards walking the top walls would have somewhere to relieve themselves. There are holes under the

This medieval cesspit was excavated at West Cotton near Raunds during the 1980s. (Northamptonshire County Council Archaeology Dept.)

privy seats which could have been used for lead pipes from a tank in the roof so that the system could have been flushed out whenever it rained. In siege situations the castle would have needed to hold out for some time, and without decent privies the occupants simply would not have lasted long.

Evidence of another county privy dating from the 12th century was found by Northamptonshire County Council's Archaeology Department at West Cotton just outside Raunds during the 1980s. Archaeologist Andy Chapman says a well built, stone-lined cesspit or garderobe was found on the site of the medieval settlement, to the north of the kitchen and bakehouse at the manor house. The discovery came as something of a surprise, as privies were not common in small rural houses of this age. It is not clear if the privy was screened by a single wall, or more fully enclosed to provide a roofed structure.

11

At the old rectory at Blisworth there is a cupboard in the wall, made especially for a chamber pot.

In the 15th and 16th centuries the better-off members of society made do with close-stools or commodes, often disguised with rich materials and with ornate wooden seats. Henry VIII kept his in a private room off the state bedchamber known as the stool room, and his pewter pot was emptied by the influential groom of the stool. Records show that Sir William Dudley of Clopton, who went bankrupt in 1730, afforded himself the

12

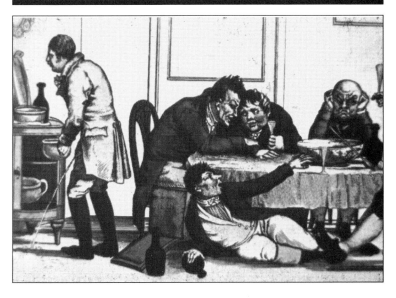

Men would think nothing of relieving themselves in public . . .

comfort of a close-stool. His belongings included a walnut tree 'necessary chair' with silk cushions, valued at 12 shillings. Sir William was the only one in the household who enjoyed such luxury, as the rest had to make do with chamber pots, which had come into common usage by this time.

At the old rectory at Blisworth there is a cupboard in a wall made especially for a chamber pot. When guests assembled for dinner parties the men would leave the table, take out the chamber pot and gather round it behind a screen. They would often quite happily continue their conversations with those at the table whilst using the pot. A similar cupboard can be found at Canons Ashby house, where it is said that men also used to relieve themselves into the fireplaces. In recent years 50 chamber pots from the Althorp estate went on the market, and now probably serve more decorative purposes.

13

Towards the end of the 16th century the very first type of water closet was created by Queen Elizabeth's godson Sir John Harington, and the Queen had one installed at Richmond Palace. The first patent on a valve water closet was taken out by a watchmaker, Alexander Cummings, in 1775. During the next few years indoor water closets were installed in many large country houses.

Poorer people, however, were still having to manage without any sanitary facilities. In the crowded streets of Northampton, people would use their chamber pots at night and then throw the contents out into the street below in the morning. Woe betide anyone who happened to be passing at the time. It is said that 'gardy-loo' (gardez-l'eau) was shouted out when a foul-smelling pail was emptied into the alleyway below, which translates as 'watch out for the water'. Records show that the Peacock Inn in Northampton had no less than 24 chamber pots to empty every morning, although it is thought that some of these may have been tipped into the dung heaps in the stables. Disease at this time was rife, with raw sewage running through the streets and mixing with the general water supplies. In the villages, people were able to be more resourceful, making good use of fields and woodlands or, if in a hurry, their own back garden. It was during the mid 18th century that the new interest in indoor facilities amongst the upper classes lost favour, and once again the great outdoors was considered the best place for doing what comes naturally. Outhouses were all the rage, and it was considered far more hygienic for sanitary facilities to be well away from the dwelling. One of Northampton's oldest surviving buildings, Welsh House in Market Square (now Dillons bookshop), certainly had an outside privy which was shown in plans of 1760. The two-holer was situated next to the coal house about 100 yards from the main house. This was a fairly common arrangement, possibly to save ladies' blushes by giving them another

Welsh House as it looked in the 1830s, from a drawing by George Clarke. Plans dating back to 1760 show an outside privy next to the coal house.

reason to pay a visit to the end of the garden. Welsh House dates back to 1595 and is one of the few town centre buildings to survive the great fire of Northampton in 1675.

A major breakthrough in hygiene came in 1848 when a public health act was passed making it law that some form of fixed sanitary arrangement must be fitted to every household. This followed a great campaign from Edwin Chadwick and other reformers. Mr Chadwick and his followers fought for change after visiting homes of the poor, many of whom lived in filthy, putrid smelling conditions, reporting that the sick could not leave their homes to dispose of their own excreta. It was said that Mr Chadwick had to visit these homes with a handkerchief covering his nose because of the foul odours and would need to hang his head out of windows to avoid being sick.

15

This lavatory pan, on display at Northampton's Abington Park Museum, dates back to the mid 19th century. A metal plate closed off the base of the pan after use, but without the modern water trap it would not have been very hygienic.

The earth closets of rural areas offered more hygienic facilities and shelter and a certain degree of privacy for the user. Deep pits were dug and a construction built over them, complete with wooden seat. The most primitive ones were just a rough plank of wood with a sawn out central hole at ground level, but gradually they were often replaced with raised wooden seats which must have seemed the height of comfort, particularly for the elderly. The Reverend Moule's patented 'pull up' earth closet, invented around 1860, released one and a half pints of earth each time it was used. One of these was removed from Blisworth House in Blisworth in spring 1997. The wooden seat was hinged to allow greater ease of cleaning and it is all in pretty good condition considering its age and use.

This Moule's earth system was removed from Blisworth House in 1997. It released 1½ pints of earth each time the closet was used. (George Freeston)

Parker's Patent 'Woodstock' Earth Closet – an improvement on Moule's closet since it was fully automatic. When the user rose the removal of pressure activated levers which dropped the earth or ashes from a hopper into the bucket.

18

An early privy bucket.

It was not until the early 20th century that a much more effi-
cient and hygienic variation was introduced when buckets were
used in the pit below the seat. The pits were either concreted
over or filled in with earth before the placing of the bucket.
Seats were hinged so that buckets could be removed when they
needed emptying. The new-style conveniences were popular
because they were less pongy and draughty, but they did have
the annoying tendency to freeze up in icy conditions.

Although flushing lavatories had actually been invented and
ignored 200 years previously, it was the Victorian sanitation
engineers who rediscovered and modified the design. Some of

19

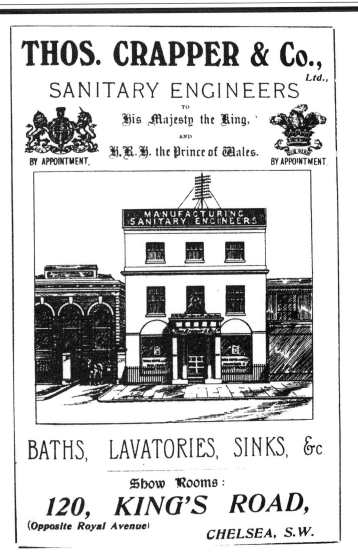

Crapper's success enabled him to open showrooms in King's Road, Chelsea.

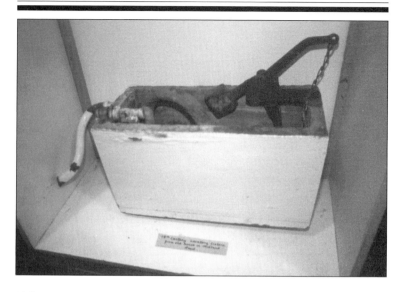

19th-century lavatory cistern removed from a house in Midland Road, Wellingborough. This is displayed in Wellingborough Heritage Centre.

them are remembered even now: Sir Henry Doulton, Thomas Twyford, Mr Shanks and, of course, Thomas Crapper, the last perfecting the water cistern with 'Crapper's Valveless Waste Preventer'. The Americans took Mr Crapper's name back to their homeland after World War 1 – and it still lives on.

In 1884 Sir Henry Doulton installed great earthenware urinals at the International Exhibition of Hygiene in London and visitors were invited to try them out free of charge. There was also a competition to find the best flushing water closet. This involved placing ten small potatoes, a sponge and four sheets of thin paper down each of the thirty pans and checking to see if all could be removed with only one flush. Only three passed the test.

However, despite all this new technology, only the most fortunate, and richest, people in Northampton were able to have water from a tap in their kitchens, connected to a main water supply. Most people had to rely on pumping water from a well, which was usually shared with others in the same street. The idea of having a flushing lavatory would have been completely out of the question. It was not uncommon for these wells to become contaminated with sewage, which inevitably caused disease and sometimes death, particularly amongst the most vulnerable such as babies, children and the elderly. Until 1875 Northampton's drains and sewers all discharged into the river Nene at South Bridge. In 1849 there was an outbreak of cholera, with 43 people dying in Northampton. Of these, all but two people lived in poor conditions in the low lying part of Bridge Street near the river. Conditions slowly improved, and a second public health act was introduced in 1875, with councils having to appoint a medical officer for health. Following on from this councils were encouraged to build sewers, street drainage, reservoirs and public lavatories, although it was still some time before many Northamptonshire villagers could see the benefits.

Generally, sewers were not laid in some rural areas until the 1940s, although there were exceptions. Greens Norton, for instance, had a sewerage system installed during World War I, albeit limited. This served houses along the main streets but others had to do without. It is said that the men digging the trenches for the sewer pipes were unhappy with their pay of fourpence an hour and went on strike. They were victorious and were given a hefty pay rise of another halfpenny an hour. Welford villagers had the benefits of a sewerage system in the late 1920s. Not so fortunate were those in Grendon, as the village was not connected to the main system until 1957, and until then most residents made do with septic tanks and the primitive privy.

It is not thought that any privies remain in use today, but there was one in the Semilong area of Northampton used as

This privy is probably Northampton's most recently used 'convenience'. It was the sole facility for an elderly gentleman in Semilong, Northampton, up to 1986. (Picture courtesy of Abington Park Museum, Northampton)

recently as 1986. It was used by a gentleman in his eighties, and it is believed that he had to resort to legal action to persuade his elderly landlord to install a modern WC. A picture of this privy is on display at the Abington Park Museum in Northampton.

[2]

TYPES OF PRIVY

Privies come in all shapes and sizes, some beautifully ornate whilst others are purely functional. Some were single seaters, whilst others were made for communal use. It was not uncommon to have two, three or even four holes cut into the seat, frequently with a little short one at the end for a child so that the whole family could use the privy at the same time. The county record seems to be a five-holer which came from the Spencer estate at Althorp, and which ended up in the garden of local historian George Freeston at Blisworth 15 years ago. Sadly, this spectacular object has long since rotted away, and all that remains is the rather grand ventilation fan which now adorns the shed in Mr Freeston's garden.

The seats were inevitably wooden, and Paul Forsythe of Irchester remembers that this did, at least, make one part of the privy fairly warm. Maureen Wright of Bugbrook remembers the wooden seat at her grandmother's privy being endlessly scrubbed: 'It is amazing that wood would take that amount of scrubbing, and the privy would always smell clean,' she said. Mary Butcher of Nether Heyford agreed. She added: 'They did lots of scrubbing and kept it very clean, the wood was as smooth as anything.'

To combat any dubious odours which could linger, sweet-smelling plants were often planted close to the privy, with lavender, roses and honeysuckle being popular choices. Big bushes planted strategically also helped to camouflage the building and give a little more privacy to the user. Early privies were made of stone and sometimes patched with wattle. Those remaining today in Northamptonshire are generally quite

The fan on the top of this shed is all that survives of a five-seater from the Spencer estate at Althorp. It now sits in a garden in Blisworth.

26

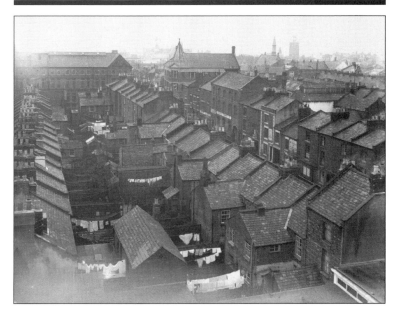

A privy block can be seen in the foreground of this picture taken in Northampton in the 1920s.

attractive and often covered with ivy. Later models were brick-built and more utilitarian, although some have their own certain charm.

Often one privy would have to cater for several houses, commonly a row of terraced cottages. Here people could find themselves getting to know their neighbours rather better than they might have liked. Although the idea of sharing lavatories today seems rather strange, it does appear that people in this situation often found the whole thing quite amenable, and a good opportunity to chat about the happenings of the day. These two or three-holers and the single-seaters generally had no locks on the door, so the more bashful would need to sing or whistle loudly to warn others of their whereabouts.

27

Another variation is two privies back to back within one building with a door at each end and divided by a thin partition. Colin Wakelin of Blisworth remembers a family one at Gayton: 'There was no soundproofing, so you certainly knew what was happening the other side.' Mr Wakelin says this particular privy was stone, with an odd bit of brickwork and an old tiled roof, and was sited about 25 yards from the house. An elderly Irthlingborough resident talks of a childhood visit to the privy at the end of the lane when her little legs didn't reach the floor. To pass the time she swung her legs, drumming her heels on the side of the 'box' and was alarmed when she heard a bellow from the other side of the partition, 'Stop kicking your heels in there, you'll go through the wood!' She added: 'Nothing was private.'

Some privies were yards away from the back door, but others were sited rather more inconveniently. Hilda Britten, now 89, was born in High Street, Irthlingborough, and remembers having a long trot right down to the bottom of her garden, around a bend and then some way down another row. She recalled: 'It certainly wasn't very nice in the rain and during winter as it was ever so cold. At night it was quite eerie and we had to use a candle. We were fortunate in one way though because the privy was our own, quite a lot of people had to share.' Mrs Britten had her first flushed loo in Coronation Year, 1953, when she moved to a house in Crow Hill. Another Irthlingborough resident who lived in Bigley's Yard, was not so lucky and had to share a privy some way up the yard: 'The worst aspect of its position was that men coming from the Vine public house knew it was there and would make their way behind three of the houses in Vine Yard to use our toilet. It wasn't always left very nice either and our mum hated cleaning it then.'

One of the most attractive privies in Northamptonshire still remains intact at the home of Mrs Bobby Deighton at Mears Ashby. Her beautifully restored stone cottage in Manor Lane

This attractive privy at Mears Ashby is a single-seater, and probably dates back to 1759.

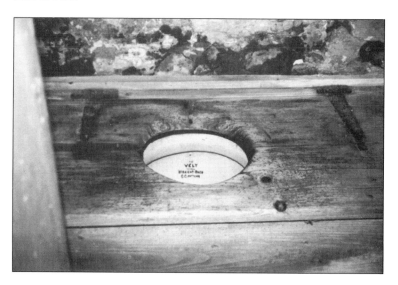

was built in 1759, and it is probable that the outside privy dates from the same period. The privy is shaped like a turret and slopes to the rear, so that it makes an unusual and interesting garden feature. Inside there is a wooden seat with a single bowl inscribed 'The Vely registered straight back CC pattern', and not surprisingly there is no flush facility as it is not connected to the sewer. Mrs Deighton and her late husband bought the former coachman's house in 1969 after 400 people had inspected and then rejected it, alarmed at all the work needed to transform it from a wreck. Mrs Deighton said: 'Before we moved in, the privy was shared by two cottages and people had to walk some way round the building to reach the back yard. It is hard to believe how awful that must have been. People had to take a bucket of water with them each time.' Mrs Deighton was told the story of two former occupants who didn't always appreciate having to share this facility: 'The old lady who lived next door spent rather a long time in the privy, and because her neighbour thought she had been in there too long, she threw open the door and threw a bucket of water at her!'

Of course, the few remaining privies in Northamptonshire have deteriorated through time and wear, but it is possible to see how the interior functional part would have looked in pristine condition from a catalogue of A. Bell & Co Ltd of Northampton. This Kingsthorpe Road company, which is still in business, had a natty line in earth closets, as depicted in a beautifully illustrated price list dating back to between 1920 and 1926. Model 1B, priced at £2 12 shillings, is described thus: 'The apparatus is operated by pulling up a Plug fixed in seat of Closet which throws out a charge of earth. The Plug and Rim under the seat are of Galvanised Iron. It is sent out on four legs, with seat fixed ready for encasing. The seat is 3ft. long, but can be cut to any other length. Total depth, back to front, 2ft. 3½ in.' The pricier Model 3A, at £3 8s 6d, boasted a novel feature: 'Is

EARTH CLOSETS.

No. 3A.

Is self-acting, the charge of earth being automatically thrown out on the user of the closet rising from the seat. Sent out on bearers fixed ready for encasing. Seat 1ft. 10in. long. Total depth, back to front, 2ft. 3½in.

Price £3 8 6

If with Earthenware Rim in place of Galvanised Iron, 6/- each extra.

No. 1B.

The above apparatus is operated by pulling up a Plug fixed in seat of Closet which throws out a charge of earth. The Plug and Rim under the seat are of Galvanised Iron. It is sent out on four legs, with seat fixed ready for encasing. The seat is 3ft. long, but can be cut to any other length. Total depth, back to front, 2ft. 3½in.

Price £2 12 0

Pull-out Pedestal A.

With Seat and casing of Varnished Teak, complete with Pail and Brackets. Measurements, 1ft. 8in. wide; 2ft. 4in. deep, and 3ft. high. Price ... £5 9 0

If fitted with Brass Pull-up Action, fitted in Seat and Enamelled Iron Rim. Sizes 2ft. 6in. wide, 2ft. 4in. deep x 3ft. 3in. high.

Price £8 10 0

Self-Acting Pedestal C,

which automatically discharges the earth on the user rising from the seat. Fitted with Enamelled Iron Rim. Pail holds about 15 uses.

Sizes 2ft. wide, 2ft. 7in. deep, 3ft. 3in. high.

Price £8 0 0

	Width.	Depth at Back.	Length.
Earth Closet Pails			17in.
,, ,, ,,			15in.
	13in.	12in.	4/- each.
	12in.	11in.	3/9 ,,

From the price list of A. Bell & Co Ltd of Northampton dated 1920-1926.

31

EARTH CLOSET TANKS ON WHEELS.

No. 1	1ft. 6in. x 1ft. 1in. x 1ft. 6in. high	...	...	...	...	...	...	...	...	£1	6	0
No. 2	2ft. x 1ft. 6in. x 1ft. 9in.	,,	.	...	...	...	.	...	..	1	8	0
No. 3	2ft. 6in. x 1ft. 4in. x 1ft. 9in. ,,	...	...	...	.	...	...	...	..	1	10	0

If without Wheels—

No. 1	...	...	...	...	...	...	...	...	...	.	...	...	...	£1	1	0
No. 2	...	...	...	...	...	...	...	.	...	..	..	...	1	2	6
No. 3	...	...	...	...	...	...	.	...	...	...	...	1	5	0

"YEARSLEY'S" PATENT GULLEY CLEANER.

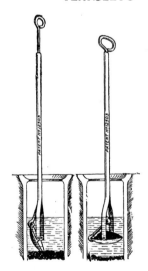

An excellent and most handy Scoop for Cleaning out Gulleys. The drawing fully explains its action.

Price ... . **2/6 each.**

From the price list of A. Bell & Co Ltd of Northampton dated 1920-1926.

self-acting, the charge of earth being automatically thrown out on the user of the closet rising from the seat.' The company also sold earth closet tanks on wheels starting at £1 6 shillings. These would have only had limited appeal because the design and construction of many local privies would have made them impossible to use in most cases. A. Bell & Co was established in 1898 by Ablett Bell and is still a family owned company. Manager John Kirkham said a lot of business in the early days was done in the villages, especially with the big estates where items would be purchased for the workers' cottages.

Privies themselves may now be in short supply, but a great many people have clear memories of what they were like. Leslie Atkins of Boughton Green Road, Northampton, remembers his childhood in the early part of the century when he visited his grandparents in Spratton at weekends. He recalls: 'The privies were down the bottom of the garden, a good 20 yard walk, which was not nice in the dark. It consisted of a wooden box seat, one high and one low for a child. Underneath was just a hole in the ground. Every time we used it we would get a little copper shovel and put down ashes mixed with lime from the builders. It was a queer do.'

Mary Gardner of New Duston, Northampton, was born in a little cottage in Duston and vividly remembers those days. She says: 'The privy, or more commonly called by us "the lavvy", was at the end of a blue brick path and adjoined the washhouse. The lavvy, which was a brick and slate building, was modestly hidden from the house by a large lilac bush. The loo itself was a large wooden boxed-in affair right across the back of the building, and as the hole had been cut right in the centre of the top, there was plenty of room for the inevitable pile of newspaper squares, comics, books and even the occasional cup of tea. Children were allowed to drum their heels on the front of the box, but over-enthusiastic drumming often had my knickers falling right off. This didn't matter on dry days, but wet weather meant a very wet floor. My brother and I, like so many siblings, were always arguing and fighting and a favourite revenge was to throw the other's possessions down the privy. This led to many a punishment, as, of course, anything thrown down there was lost for ever.'

Recollections also come from Jackie Atkins of Hinton Road, Northampton, who remembers with mixed feelings her gran's outside water closet in Melbourne Street, Northampton, which was used until it was demolished in 1975. 'The brick building was attached to the house and the loo was a wooden bench seat with a hole and a ceramic bowl. There was no plumbing of any sort, flushing was done by a bucket of water. There were no lights either so a candle was always needed on dark nights and if it was windy that was usually blown out before you reached the loo so a box of matches was always left out there. When I was young I thought it was quite a novelty, but as I got older I changed my mind. Many people couldn't believe that my gran still had such a loo in the seventies, but she never minded.'

Of course, many people alive today have memories of using privies. A Northampton resident, 78-year-old Frances Staughton of Forfar Street, can recall her childhood when she lived in a quaint thatched cottage in The Riding, leading off Fish Street, in the 1920s. 'We lived in a house built from the stone from the castle. No tap, no loo, no windows on the back of the house. We got our fresh water from a tap facing our house.' Mrs Staughton remembers having to trek to privies in adjacent streets, one where the Co-op arcade now stands and another in Grooms Yard where there was just a wooden seat over a hole.

A privy in Sunderland Street, Northampton, between the years 1913 and 1936 is vividly remembered by Renee Creek. The 83-year-old, who still lives in the town, said the privy was built at the end of the house and was connected to the sewer.

The outside privy meant for servants still exists in a basement next door to the Royal Theatre in Guildhall Road, Northampton. The building used to be a private house before being taken over as additional space for theatre staff, with the basement used as the wardrobe department. The original water closet has long gone, but its replacement is still in daily use.

She recalls: 'It was a white wooden seating structure, scrubbed down every Monday with the washday suds. It had a deep funnelled enamelled white pan and the bench each side was wide enough for candle and matches to be put there. There was a small hook behind the door for coat or mac for bad weather and a small hook for pieces of newspaper. In winter, if snow was expected – and we were a good judge of the weather in those days – mother would say "Better put the brush at the top of the yard". If it snowed you needed to sweep the snow making a path to the privy.' A galvanised bucket with rainwater from the garden tub was used to pour down the pan, and this together with plenty of disinfectant did a good job of preventing bad smells. Mrs Creek again had to make do with outside facilities when she was

35

married and living in Stanley Road from 1942. She remembers the excitement of choosing a rose pink toilet for a bathroom extension in 1975 and says it felt so posh after all those years of an outside privy. 'I feel so comfortable and blessed with modern conveniences,' she adds.

Conditions in the county's villages in the 1920s were much the same, as Betty Soames from Knox Road, Wellingborough, remembers. As a young girl she lived in Grendon where four privies were located at the end of a very long yard, and had to be shared by the occupants of six houses. 'The one we shared had two holes in the seat, one large and one small, obviously a family affair, catering for all sizes. Although nowadays people would think that was carrying togetherness a bit too far, in those days we took it in our stride. Life in those days was very simple but I can't remember feeling deprived because I didn't have a chain to pull. In fact I don't think I knew that there were such things. With no electricity, no running water and primitive privies which left a lot to be desired it is a wonder we didn't all succumb to some dreadful disease, but we were hardy souls and lived to tell the tale.'

Meg Goatly of Brigstock remembers the privy at her home in Loddington between 1918 and 1926. 'It was way across the garden, next to the wash-house – brick built with a red tiled floor. It was a white scrubbed wooden privy complete with one-holer with oval shaped bucket. This was no water privy, and a bucket of ashes or dry earth and a shovel was kept besides to be sprinkled on after use.'

Jack Grazier, aged 78, of Woodford Halse describes his childhood privy as a masterpiece of architectural design: 'The building was divided into two sections, one with a large opening for the depositing of ashes from fires which in turn helped to cover the deposits from the toilet next door. The toilet was entered by a three-quarters length door with a large gap top and bottom. The toilet itself consisted of a brick wall with a lower portion at one end for juniors. This was topped with a wooden seat for two adults and one child.'

Stan Houghton has lived in Irthlingborough for most of his life, and spent his childhood in a terraced house in Lime Terrace. He says there are still spaces in the outside walls where people used to keep the buckets for flushing out the outside privies. Mr Houghton remembers the pantiled building, also containing a coal barn and a utility room, adjoined to a similar place for next-door neighbours: 'The two utility places were in the middle, and at the end there were long, narrow toilets with wooden hinged box seats. I remember sitting there and looking through the rafters at the chinks of light.'

[3]

STORIES FROM AROUND NORTHAMPTONSHIRE

Lavatory humour was very much in evidence in bygone years. It seems that the privy lent itself well to creating entertainment for many. Unfortunately, usually at the expense of the user. Iris Sanders of Hackleton spent her childhood in Piddington where her father was the village blacksmith. She remembers having to use a bucket in the kitchen, an arrangement which would definitely not meet with approval from health and hygiene inspectors nowadays. Mrs Sanders remembers the exploits of mischievous young children, herself included: 'There was a row of seven houses at an angle to the road. On the right hand side there were steps to a brick built loo on the edge of the road, which was used by an old boy. He had a padlock on it. The roof was level with the steps, so we kids would wait until he came home from work and went to the loo. One of the lads would quietly creep up and put the chain back over the lock, then he would get onto the roof and start jumping and dancing. The old boy would shout and swear. All went quiet. He would shout "Let me out!" The lad would eventually creep round and loosen the chain and sit back behind the hedge with the rest of us.' Apparently the long-suffering chap used to take all this in good part. 'He was a good natured man,' Mrs Sanders recalls. A story about another resident of the same row of houses was told to Mrs Sanders by her father: 'A woman bought a wooden, portable loo, which was really super compared to the rest. One day some lads waited until she was inside, tied rope round it and lifted it off the ground. They carried it to the allotment and this woman just couldn't believe what had happened.'

Youngsters often found privies a source of amusement. This picture shows children playing in St James Square, Northampton, in the 1930s.

There is another fearful tale told about a Yardley Gobion resident aged around ten years in 1960 who had best remain anonymous. The story involves a poor woman who had a proper earth closet at the bottom of her garden, with a rear opening onto an alleyway at the back. This boy and his friends would wait until she got inside and was sitting down. They would then creep up behind the door at the rear and shove nettles in, which they would move around and then beat a hasty retreat. Such indignity, not to mention pain.

A Cranford resident, 91-year-old Bernard James, still remembers an incident which happened in the village in the 1920s. Mr James has lived there all of his life but will never forget the day he inadvertently caused an odorous mystery in the village: 'My father was the blacksmith and we lived in Cranford St Andrews. We had a brick built square place in the back yard, about six foot square by four foot high. This is where we put the fire ashes and when it was time to empty the buckets we would drain away the liquid and put solids into the ashes. Then when this was full it was put into a wheelbarrow and spread about the garden. We were a big family, there were seven children and two adults, so the buckets very quickly got filled.

'I remember a time when I was a teenager and my father was ill in bed so mother told me that it would have to be my job to empty the full buckets into the ashes at the blacksmith's yard. This meant carrying them right along the street, so it was a job best done after dark. There were no street lights in those days, torches were not invented so what we had was a candle in a lantern. I brought the bucket down the entry between the two houses and was walking down past the reading rooms (now the village hall). When I got to the bottom of The Green the door opened and I suddenly remembered there was a whist drive that evening and they were all coming out. I thought "Oh no, what do I do now? Do I make a dash for it?" I made a dash and slipped over and the bucket rolled away, spreading the contents everywhere. People were coming out of the room and saying "Oh what an unpleasant stink" and "Isn't it slippery along here". I managed to find the bucket and took it back to my mother. She said "You are quicker than your father." I told her what had happened and she got me up at 7 am the next morning to get out and clear it up. It had all dried out, and all I could do was shovel up the bits of used newspaper which were lying along the lane.'

Because of their rural locations, some village privies attracted occupants other than human. Dorothy Dunn of The Oval, Kettering, remembers living in Burton Latimer in the 1960s as a newly-wed. She said: 'I was living in a block of six houses and there was only one privy between the families. While in there one day I heard someone banging on the door. I called "Wait a minute" but they kept on. Thinking they must be desperate I opened the door to find a pig there! It had come from the farm across the road and up the entry.'

On the subject of pigs, 97-year-old Mrs Thompson of Hartwell remembers the discomfort of visiting her friend's privy a long way from the house which was located next to the pig sty: 'It was quite a hazard on a wet dark night wondering which door one was going to use!' Mrs Thompson also recalls having to take an umbrella with her to the privy whenever it rained because there was a hole in the roof at the most inappropriate place.

Local historian George Freeston took this photograph of the privy at his Blisworth home before it was demolished.

As a child, Brenda Faulkner lived in a house next to a wood yard in Regent Street, Kettering. She remembers the house had virtually no garden, and the privy was about 100 yards from the back door. 'The privy itself was boxed in, had an enamel bowl like a proper toilet, but the only problem was that we had no chain to pull. My mother and members of the family had to make sure there was a constant supply of water waiting there to flush the contents straight into the sewer. As my brother, sister and I were growing up we invited friends round and some of them were not used to a privy so my father used to play a joke on them. When leaving the back door he used to call out to them "Now don't forget to pull the chain m'duck" and as we had no electricity in the privy our friends couldn't see properly. After finishing their business and remembering the words my father had spoken, they started fumbling for the chain to flush. Then they would come out with a certain look of embarrassment on their face. As we knew the joke about the chain we stood around laughing our heads off.' Mrs Faulkner remembers that the family got so fed up with not having a flushable lavatory that they took drastic action. One bitterly cold freezing night Mrs Faulkner's mother sneakily fetched a hammer and gave a swift blow to the pan. She then notified the landlord that the frost had cracked the pan and it was unfit for use. The family tentatively suggested one with a chain, and were thrilled when they realised that the replacement had a modern flushing device.

Tampering with a privy gave David Dodd of Kettering a sleepless night. He tells of a two-seater at his home in Cottingham during the 1940s where a candle and box of matches were usually to be found to the rear of the seat to lighten the darkness. He said: 'I can recall one night in the pursuit of scientific learning and idle curiosity, deliberately dropping a lighted match

43

down there. It set light to a piece of newspaper which was stick-ing up above the general wet mess. Attempts to pee on it proved unsuccessful, so with no more wee wees left I retreated back to the house to observe from my bedroom window. Having recently been told at school about methane gas I spent half the night expecting a huge explosion, but eventually fell asleep. A quick check in the morning revealed the privy was still standing, just as it had been for the last half century.'

Andrew Clare of Far Cotton, Northampton, remembers the 'thunder-box' situated at the bottom of the garden when he was living in a two-up, two-down in Oxford Street, demolished in the late 1960s. His mother was scared by mice and rats lurking in the privy, so before any visit he would quickly open the door and throw the cat in, and wait a few moments before entering. Mr Clare remembers how his father's good DIY skills and ingenuity came in handy. 'Not long after moving in my Dad laid on water to the loo, but the system was continually being blocked by birds or mice. On a regular cleaning mission, Mum stood on the thun-der-box, slipped and fell, breaking the already woodwormed seat. To make a new one, not too big or too small, Dad got Mum to talc her bum and sit on a piece of wood. I had to get a wet bum and sit on it afterwards.' The perfect sized hole was then created, slightly bigger than Mr Clare's imprint and a little smaller than his mother's.

On the same subject, an elderly Irchester resident's method was to remove his bowler hat and cut around that.

When septic tanks were introduced, they were seen as an improvement on the pit arrangement, but they did have their own problems. John Bass of Long Buckby said it was a common occurrence for people to put a dead rabbit or cat into the tank to get the mix right: 'You were told by the council people to do this, because what you were aiming for was to get a crud on top because then there was no smell.'

Dogs and outside privies do not always mix, as Police Officer Peter Eads of Northampton recalls. He was posted to Irchester immediately after the war in the 1940s and found lodgings in Farndish Road where the lavatory was sited at the bottom of the garden. 'In those days when stray dogs came my way on the beat I had to walk them to the kennels at Wellingborough or Rushden police stations. Out late one night I came across a very nice golden labrador; much too late for the long trek, I took it back to the digs and tied it securely to the lavatory door. Much to the horror of my landlady she discovered the next morning that a very playful dog had chewed the bottom boards of the lavatory door away. She threatened immediate expulsion of the dog and myself. To cut a long story short, the Police Authority provided a new door and I became her favourite lodger.'

In Northamptonshire privies were called by all sorts of names (see 'A Privy by Any Other Name'), but one Northampton lady remembers how she was confused when first moving to the county from London in the 1940s. 'We had always called it the closet, so when I moved to lodgings here and my landlady told me to put all my clothes in the closet I was quite upset. I thought "I'm not living here".'

45

[4]

PARTICULAR PRIVIES

LONG BUCKBY

A fine example of a traditional privy can be seen at Corner
House in Long Buckby where a quaint ivy-covered stone building nestles at the foot of the garden. The building boasts a
wooden three-seater and was emptied from the rear. Owner
and former psychiatric nurse John Bass has lived in the 17th-cen-
tury house for several years with his wife and three former residents of St Crispin's at Duston. Mr Bass describes the privy as
being 'in a nice state of dereliction' and says if it were smartened

John Bass at the doorway to his privy at Corner House, Long Buckby. It was
last used in the 1930s and is described as being 'in a nice state of dereliction'.

up it would lose all its atmosphere. The building has six-inch thick walls and feels strangely snug and silent inside. It is so soundproofed that you cannot even hear rain falling outside. One of the occupants of Corner House has a definite fondness for the building and enjoys shutting himself inside and lying across the wooden seats. The last person to recall using this particular privy was former occupier Richard Tebbutt who still lives in Long Buckby. He said: 'I remember using it in the 1930s when I was a child. There were privies in the house then, but we used this one when we were outside. It was emptied once a year and there was quite a smell.'

Mr Bass remembers having to make do with outside facilities himself when he moved to a cottage in Harpole in 1969. 'We had been used to modern comforts but suddenly only had a toilet under a lilac tree in the garden. We had to manage for 18 months until we had planning permission to convert an annexe on the end of the house.' Mr Bass says the regular bucket emptying was the most inconvenient aspect: 'I was a good singer and had been roped into the Boys Brigade to train the band. It was my first parade and I was in a rush to get there, but I was desperate to go to the toilet and the bucket was full. I had to rush about digging holes and emptying this thing, whilst all the time still wanting to go badly.'

BLISWORTH

Another three-seater still exists tucked away in an outhouse at Hill Farm in Blisworth. Farmer Colin Wakelin said he was interested to discover the privy when moving to the property many years ago, and has no intention of removing or converting the building. 'I would like to think I have helped save a little bit of history,' he said. It was thought that Hill Farm was built in the

This three-seater survives at Hill Farm, Blisworth. Two seats are for adults and there's room for a little one on the end.

1820s and the privy was almost certainly built at the same time. The building contains two adults' seats and one child's and has a pit underneath which can be emptied from the rear. The building is rather gloomy, with a tiny window letting in only a glimmer of light. Former occupants must have been delighted when water was brought into the house and flush lavatories were installed.

IRTHLINGBOROUGH

Not everyone has bad memories of their privy and Coral Alabaster of Lilley Terrace, Irthlingborough, is especially fond of hers, particularly because of its very special link with her mother. She tells of the day of her death over 35 years ago: 'Just before going

48

This former privy, now used as a coal shed, has fond memories for Coral Alabaster of Irthlingborough.

in Mother was asked by a neighbour how she was, and she replied "Never better". She never came out again but died peacefully in there.' Mrs Alabaster has happy memories of the brick-built privy when she was a child: 'I used to sit in the loo and use the base as a drum for my heels. I would sit, sing and draw to my heart's content. All my real thinking went on in there, it was so quiet and peaceful. When the toilet was taken out my heel marks were very clear on the base from years of drumming. My parents always knew where I was as they could hear the noise of my heels on the wood.' Mrs Alabaster also recalls a time during the Second World War when an evacuee got locked in the privy for about an hour, much to his annoyance and the other children's great amusement. Mrs Alabaster later returned to the house to live with her husband and again used to use the privy every evening before retiring: 'It was quite pleasant

49

to have a walk down the yard with the stars shining overhead, having a nice quiet sit and then going to bed.' Eventually the lavatory was replaced with one indoors, but the building still serves a useful purpose as a coal shed. Mrs Alabaster believes that she may one day restore the privy to its original use and would quite look forward to her moonlit walks again.

There is another Irthlingborough story told by a former Addington Road resident about how a privy became a refuge one bright moonlit night in 1940: 'A German plane dropped a stick of bombs up the by-pass. Father had gone to bed, but had seen a flare at the bottom of the road and went downstairs to see what was happening. He went out to the wall and realised a bomb had exploded on the pumphouse below the workhouse – another at the end of the front steps, another in the middle of the main road and more up the allotments. Realising the danger, he rushed into the lavatory. Chunks of shrapnel went through the door and fractured the water pipe above the lavatory. The holes in the door were still there when the houses were finally pulled down.'

GREAT BILLING

A two-seater privy remains intact, but a little worse for wear, within the conservation area of Great Billing. The building is tucked away in a corner of a garden and was originally built of stone, but has been patched up with bricks in recent years. The wooden seat with two holes survives, and owner Julie Martell has no intention of making any changes, describing the privy as 'a little piece of history'. Mrs Martell believes the privy was probably used up to the late 1930s when the house was linked up to the water system. However, in more recent years it served very nicely as a playhouse for Mrs Martell's children.

This two-seater privy survives in Great Billing. Ashes can be seen when peering down into the depths.

LONG BUCKBY AGAIN . . .

Another two-seater survives in Kings Street, Long Buckby, at the home of Jacqui Butlin. It seems that this was once a three-seater, as there is evidence that there was also a small child's seat at an angle to the adult seats. Mrs Butlin and her husband consider the privy an unusual garden feature, and have plans to restore it to its former glory some time in the future. The brick-built privy has a slate roof and is just a short walk from the 18th century house, although Mrs Butlin believes that it may have been added when building work was carried out in 1886. The privy was last used a century later on 10th December 1986, the day the Butlin family moved into their home. 'When one of the removal men asked me where the lavatory was, I jokingly

This privy in Long Buckby is thought to date back to 1886. It was originally a three-seater, but only two seats remain.

Jacqui Butlin outside her privy at Long Buckby.

told him that he would have to use the privy. To our amusement, he actually did so,' recalls Mrs Butlin.

... AND AGAIN

Also in Kings Street, there is evidence that outside lavatories were still being built in the 1930s, even though the trend was for new homes to have indoor loos. The small brick building is set in the middle of Mrs Bigley's garden and has a full flush lavatory, although it has not been used for well over 30 years. It seems surprising that when the terraced row of houses were being constructed the builders decided that the lavatory

Emily Bigley outside her privy at Long Buckby. It was built in the 1930s and now serves a useful function as a shed.

should be located inconveniently down the garden instead of inside or adjacent to the house.

[5]

WHEN NEWSPAPERS WERE NOT JUST
FOR READING

Nowadays we are able to enjoy the luxury of soft tissue paper, conveniently on hand in an array of pastel shades or even padded for extra comfort. We reach out and tear off the required length without a moment's thought, but this was not always so.

The Romans, who were way ahead of us in such matters, devised a method of cleansing by using a small stick with a sponge attached to the end. These would be placed in public lavatories and after use the sponge would be rinsed out in salt water, ready for the next person. It is believed that this practice was the origin for the expression 'to get hold of the wrong end of the stick'.

Before privies were in common use and when people just sat down behind a bush to answer a call of nature, they used the first thing on hand such as bunches of hay and grass, smooth stones and leaves. Wet grass was considered to be particularly good for the task. It is also thought that mussel shells were used by those living near the coast. The earliest toilet rolls were actually available from 1880 when the British Patent Perforated Paper Company began to manufacture shiny greaseproof type paper such as Izal and Bronco. However, for some peculiar reason, toilet paper did not become popular until many years later. Instead, in Northamptonshire as elsewhere, people favoured newspaper squares to do the job. By the turn of the century, before the advent of television, newspapers were considered essential for most households, so were in plentiful supply. Comics and magazines were also used, but the shinier surface was thought to be too slippery to do a thorough job.

The editions featuring portraits of Hitler were particularly popular . . .

Walter Clements, aged 88, who has lived in Wellingborough all his life, says the newspapers were cut into rectangles approximately six inches by seven inches and then strung together with a piece of string. He personally favoured *The Times* and the *Guardian*. However, the favourites were local papers such as the *Northampton Chronicle* or the *Mercury & Herald*, the forerunner of today's *Chronicle & Echo* and *Northampton Mercury*. Renee Creek of St James, Northampton, recalls: 'It was a popular conversation as to which was the best – durable and soft as possible. The local papers were the favourite. My mother had a good idea to make it a bit softer. We took a piece and holding it each side, we would ruffle it between our fingers and it was more pleasant to use.' Mrs Creek remembers, as a child, wondering what the Queen used, and added: 'What a joy when soft paper was invented.' Bert Knight of Daventry recalls how, in the 1930s, he and his sister would tear up squares of the *Daily Express* and hang them on a piece of string: 'Not very hygienic and also very hard I seem to remember.'

John Bass of Long Buckby remembers using newspaper squares, but believes the print must have been of better quality in those days, because he cannot recall it coming off and leaving people with black and blue backsides. Maggie Lyons of Wellingborough remembers visiting her gran's privy in Church Street, Finedon, during the 1960s. She remembers reading the newspaper squares in the privy and then being thoroughly annoyed when she was halfway through an interesting article but could never find the other half amongst the remaining squares. Bert from Northampton remembers how children used to loosen bricks in the dividing wall between two adjoining privies, making a gap and then swapping comics meant as lavatory paper. He recalls that making a mini-window like this also made chatting a lot easier.

There were few alternatives to newspaper, but a little

ingenuity went a long way and Meg Goatly of Brigstock remembers cutting up the tissue paper in which oranges were wrapped. Today, packaging goes straight into the bin without a second thought, but in years gone by it would be pounced upon with glee and put to good use.

[6]

REVOLTING RODENTS AND OTHER HORRORS

Privies were never the nicest of places, but some people's experiences were worse than others.

Betty Soames, who grew up in Grendon during the 1920s remembers being frightened of the visit to the privy: 'These long distance loos at the bottom of the yard were alright in the daytime, but woe betide anybody who wanted to "go" after dark. Coats, hats and torches had to be found, and somebody always had to accompany "the nuisance" and wait outside the doors until the mission was accomplished. With the wind rattling the slats at the bottom of the alley, and the torch making shadows on the wall, it was quite an eerie experience.' Mrs Soames' treks to the privy came to a rather abrupt end when two walls collapsed in a raging storm. The next morning she found it inhabited by curious cows and, despite enjoying fresh air, the family decided to leave the privy to its fate. Of course the very thought of sitting over a deep, dark hole made some people nervous. Mrs Soames remembers clutching the seat tightly in case she fell into the darkness below to be swept away and never seen again.

This fear of falling down the deep, dark hole came only too true in some cases. Jennifer Green of Great Harrowden remembers the chilling moment when her toddler fell into the privy. 'I was gardening peacefully and heard my two year old son crying. When I looked for him he had fallen through the hole. I had to reach down to rescue him and carry him straight to the bath.' Mrs Green also recalls her childhood at Knuston Lodge Farm at Irchester where two outside earth closets were used until the

Scene of tragedy – the former Blue Coat School at the bottom of Bridge Street, Northampton, where a young child drowned in a privy.

early 1960s. She said the south-facing lavatory was a great breeding ground for flies, which could put the privy user in a rather uncomfortable and ticklish situation. Flies were not the

60

only occupants of this particular privy, as in summer swallows would nest in there which at least gave people something interesting to look at.

Whilst Mrs Green's child was none the worse for his experience, there is a particularly distressing story about a young boy who was not so fortunate. The *Mercury & Herald* newspaper reported the death of eight year old Edward Vernon who was found dead in a privy in August 1797. Local historian George Freeston says the incident happened at the former Blue Coat School in Bridge Street, Northampton. 'The poor boy fell into a 20 foot deep hole and drowned. No-one realised he was missing and he was there for some time. It must have been like hell.' The charity school was closed in December 1921.

On a lighter note, a 75-year-old Northampton lady remembers how her neighbour's chicken fell down the privy one day. 'The bird was hauled out and washed under the communal tap, none the worse for the experience.' Some unfortunate kittens were not so lucky. Dorothy Evans of Northampton recalls a sad tale: 'Our cat had kittens and father said we had to get rid of them. My brother, who was about six at the time, went off and came back proudly a little while later saying "I've got rid of them". He had dropped them down the toilet.'

Rats were unfortunately all too common, and quite naturally the revolting rodents thrived near privies. Iris Sanders vividly remembers one horrible Saturday afternoon in the 1940s. At the time she lived with her husband and three small children in a tiny cottage in Hackleton where she shared a rather primitive back-to-back privy with several neighbours. 'My youngest child was four years old and I had taken him down to the closet. We had a big one and a little one alongside. He wanted to sit on the big one but I was a bit worried because he was very small and I thought I might lose him down it. I gave in and he sat there very still, perched up on this seat. I was standing outside and I saw the back end of a big rat go under the door. I just didn't know what to do. I knew that if I shouted then he would fall down the closet. My husband was out the back of the garden so I called to my boy, "Don't you move". I tore up the garden and told my husband to bring his spade. I said, "Sit still, Daddy is just going to hit a mouse". He killed this rat. It was a choice of letting the rat survive or risking my son falling down the closet.' Mrs Sanders had to wait until 1952 before she had a modern lavatory.

Another gruesome rat tale is told by Leslie Atkins of Northampton who recalls visiting a friend in Washington Street during the 1940s. Mr Atkins' friend had an outside privy with underneath pit which was flushed with buckets of water. He said: 'I went down to put in a pedestal pan and system but when we took out the box seat we got a surprise – there was a rats' nest directly underneath.'

Still on rats, Jackie Atkins of Northampton remembers that the vermin were the worst aspect of her gran's loo in Melbourne Street: 'Many times I have sped there and back and I remember with horror seeing a rat scurry about. To this day I can't stand them. It is amazing how quick one can do what has to be done knowing a rat might pop in.'

Mr Akred of Far Cotton, Northampton, remembers the scariness of having to visit the privy at his grandparents' cottage when he was a boy: 'On a dark and rough night it was a difficult job as we had to use a candle to find the way, and a box of matches would be used to get there and back. It was of brick construction and it was covered with ivy and one had to be careful because as you opened the door you might be confronted with a rat or birds or mice in the ivy. We had a laugh one dark winter's evening when grandfather needed to go and grandmother said "Can't you wait until the next new moon?"'

Roy Barker, from Duston, grew up in the St James area of Northampton where he had a privy connected to the sewer, but unfortunately no plumbing. He had a special technique for combating fear of hidden horrors: 'As a young boy it was a bit daunting on a dark winter's night to have to make the trip into the back yard. The trick was to make a silent approach to the lav, gently release the catch then kick the door back hard so it hit the wood. This made sure that anyone lying in wait behind that door would be put out of action.' Mr Barker also tells the story of an American visiting a village in the county who was rather amazed at the outside privy. 'He remarked that the door had no lock on it. To this, the ancient owner of the cottage said, "Well, we've never had anyone run off with that bucket yet." '

Peggy Skinner of Northampton remembers her childhood loo as having no windows, no light and being very scary. She added: 'I think it was worse for me because when I was two or three years old my aunt thought I had done something wrong and put me in her coal house which was completely dark. It seemed a long time to me but it was probably only a few minutes and from then on I was afraid of the dark.'

Extremes of weather were bad news for privy users, with hot weather increasing smells and cold weather making the trip down the garden path hard going. A Grendon resident remembers 50 or so years ago when it was necessary to trek 75 yards to the privy: 'The door was not very well fitted and you can imagine how unpleasant it was to sit there on a cold snowy day.'

Mary Gardner of New Duston describes vividly just how awful the privy trek could be for youngsters: 'As children we had to be dressed in our outdoor clothes and sent forth with a paraffin storm lantern. This was very scary on a pitch dark, wet and windy night with trees blowing about creating strange and frightening shapes and shadows, especially if the storm lantern blew out, as it often did. My brother was very fond of

63

telling me of ghosts and monsters, and I can still remember the terror of those winter evening trips, his warnings of "watch out for that ghostie" firmly in my mind. The path seemed endless and even the old lilac bush took on strange and sinister appearances. Thank goodness for modern amenities.' Indeed.

[7]

A Good Shovelful

If having to use a privy sounds unpleasant, spare a thought for the poor souls who had the unenviable task of disposing of the contents. Instead of putting out a wheely bin or black plastic bag for the refuse collectors, it was not uncommon for people in bygone years to leave out a bucket filled with sewage to be borne away.

Many older villagers in South Northants still remember a great character, Joe Hakes, who used to ride round the narrow lanes with his horse and cart, unfortunately often leaving a rather unsavoury trail and odour in his wake. One chap also vividly remembers the thick line of buzzing flies which surrounded the cart. Mr Hakes lived in Bugbrooke where the school now stands, in a tiny thatched cottage with one room downstairs and two upstairs. Maureen Wright, who lives in the village, recalls her schooldays in the late 1940s, when children would meet the cart on their way to school in the mornings. 'Quite often as we passed by, some waste would fall out of the cart, you can imagine how lovely that was.'

Joe's daughter Edna York, who still lives in Bugbrooke, vividly remembers her father going round to people's houses and collecting their buckets and emptying the contents onto his cart before disposing of it at Heyford. She said: 'Dad was a real character and a popular man. He was a jokey sort of man, you could ask anyone in Bugbrooke. He had an answer to them all. He would partially empty the buckets into people's gardens, so he didn't have to carry the liquid on his cart and he didn't care less what people thought.'

Edna, who was the eldest of eight children, says her father did

Night soil men working under cover of darkness. (from *The Complete Loo* by Roger Kilroy, Victor Gollancz, 1984)

this work all his life and recalls that money was scarce when she was young. She remembers him coming straight in the house after work and having a bath and changing his clothes before

66

he would do anything else. 'When I married at the age of 20 in 1940, I lived in a council house and I had a bucket, so I knew what it was like myself. Dad had to empty my bucket then along with all the rest. It was not very pleasant work, and the buckets were very heavy when full. They were galvanised, like old-fashioned baths. It was a hard life.'

Betty Soames of Wellingborough grew up in Grendon during the 1920s and remembers the night soil man coming to collect buckets for emptying each week. 'You can imagine the trouble it caused if he was a few days late, as buckets only hold so much of any commodity. He came with a horse and cart containing a large tank. One very hot summer's day the tank had a leak and left a trail of sewage up the hill and down the lane, the pong of which I can remember still.'

A Northampton lady whose bucket was emptied weekly in the 1930s, remembers a long suffering soul having to put up with lads singing a ditty as the task was carried out. It went:

> The corporation muck cart was filled up to the brim,
> The driver fell in backwards and found he couldn't swim.
> He struggled out in a fit
> Covered with shit.

In the third edition of *Northamptonshire Past and Present*, Colin Hughes recalls life in Ascote near Towcester in the 1930s when his mother bought the village shop: 'Up a flight of blue bricks and to the left past the top of the gardens were the closets. You could, in high summer, tell where they were with your eyes closed. They were emptied after a time by men from Towcester and the clang of the buckets being moved could be heard plainly in the lane.'

It is also recorded that there was quite an outcry in Great Addington, also in the 1930s, when the night soil remover started calling later, at around 8 am, which was considered particularly objectionable to those eating breakfast at this hour.

Going back to the turn of the century, it is believed that the contents of many buckets served a rather useful purpose to local industry. Several elderly people remembered urine being collected by tanneries for use in the leather making process, but there is no real evidence to support this. However, Dave Abbott, who is managing director of Debdale Leather Co of Finedon, believes the stories are quite likely to be true: 'I know that many years ago before the development of man-made enzymes which are used in some of the pre-tanning processes, chicken and dogs' droppings were used. There is no reason why human urine should not have been used too.' On the assumption that human offerings were in plentiful supply, but dog urine less easy to obtain, it does seem highly likely that recycling in Northampton took a very novel form.

Whilst privies with buckets obviously had to be emptied with some frequency, the pit variety were left for some time, possibly a year or more before the contents were removed. This task usually took place in the middle of the night, probably because of the smell and people's sensibilities. Sometimes a bonfire burned at the same time, probably to create a less unpleasant smell. Quite often, if the privy contents were to remain in the garden, they would be left on top of a trench to soak in, before

The rear of a privy in Long Buckby. The contents drained into a tank which then had to be emptied regularly.

the trench was filled in a couple of days later. Quite how the occupiers and others living nearby coped with this is hard to imagine. Many village properties filled their gardens in this way for many years, a practice which could explain today's rich soil in the county and its good vegetable crops. Ernie Smith of Kings Heath, Northampton, remembers the 1930s, in Penryn Road, when buckets were emptied onto the garden: 'My father used to believe this was very good for runner beans.'

Colin Wakelin of Hill Farm, Blisworth, recalls his childhood in Gayton when a local man, Ted Paul, would carry out the grim annual job: 'We had a privy way down the garden and it would be emptied once a year or so. Ted had a long handled ladle and would go round the back, remove the cover and ladle it into buckets which would then be put onto the garden. The soil at these houses became very workable type soil, and good

69

A long-handled scoop was used to empty the earth-type privies – not a job many people relished!

vegetables were grown. My grandparents had a thatched cottage in Deene's Row and there was a row of privies at the bottom. My parents always made sure I wasn't around when it was emptied.' Mr Wakelin's father kept the Eykyn Arms pub, and he remembers Ted Paul coming into the bar and regaling the regulars with stories of his exploits: 'He seemed to relish the job, and looked upon it as a kind of public service.'

Mary Garner of New Duston recalls her father emptying the pit once a year, through a small door at the back. 'This was done with a long handled scoop, usually in winter and not before the neighbours had been warned as the smell was pretty awful.' An example of the scoop Ms Garner refers to can be seen in A. Bell & Co's price list. ' "Yearsley's" Patent Gulley Cleaner' is described as: 'An excellent and most handy Scoop for Cleaning out Gulleys' (see illustration on page 32). It was priced at 2/6.

This dreadful job is also recalled by Bert Knight of Daventry who says that in the 1930s his father would go to borrow a big scoop to clear out the family two-seater. He remembers his father actually being very ill each time it had to be done.

David Dodd of Hawthorn Road, Kettering, remembers the disposal of privy contents at his childhood home in Cottingham: 'The hole in the ground was about nine feet deep and every few months it had to be emptied. This was done by removing a slab at the back and ladling the sludge into a wheelbarrow for transporting to the garden. The ladle had a wooden handle about twelve feet long, the semi-spherical spoon was about eight inches diameter. This piece of high-tech equipment was retained at the landlord's house for safe keeping. It was often my task, with the promise of a threepence reward, to fetch this implement from Mr Simpson's house in Blind Lane, about half a mile away. So, with my mother's voice singing in my ears "Be sure to carry it by the handle'', off I would go. To dispose of the sludge a trench or trenches would have been dug in someone's garden, each neighbour taking it in turn for the privilege. The men from three or four households would combine their efforts to speed up this somewhat unpleasant job; one ladling, one wheeling the barrow, one backfilling the trench and one taking a breather. They would invariably smoke cigarettes, even if they didn't normally. "Keeps the flies away lad", they would say.' Mr Dodd went on to say that this means of sewage disposal had its benefits: 'Anything planted in the ground above flourished beyond measure. Tomatoes in particular did extremely well, producing the biggest and best for many a mile around. It was an early lesson in recycling. Even at that age I could see that people ate tomatoes, sat on the privy to make more sewage, more sewage made more tomatoes, people ate the tomatoes ad infinitum.'

An 84-year-old who grew up in a large house at Naseby, complete with thatched roof and mud and wattle walls, vividly remembers privy emptying time: 'Periodically on moonlit nights the men of the household would go up with buckets and ladles on long handles and empty them in a large hole which they would have dug in the garden. We children would be walking home from choir practice or concert practice and the boys would say "Cor blimey" or some such expression maybe more vulgar. There was a terrible smell, still it was all we had in the village. Some people in Naseby did have a bucket instead which they emptied every week.'

A lady who has lived in Grendon all her life told the story of a visitor from town who was interested to see a man in the village with a horse and cart which was loaded with oil drums. The lady decided he was a mobile florist and asked to buy some flowers, and was very shocked when she realised what the contents of the oil drums actually were.

There is a sad tale about a horse and cart collecting night soil at Stanwick. Apparently the horse got out of control and started galloping down a hill, eventually drawing to an abrupt halt at the bottom when the horse and cart smashed into a wall of a house. The unfortunate occupier came downstairs to find a dead horse and the contents of the neighbourhood's privies in his home.

[8]

POTTY PONTIFICATIONS

Trips to the privy when darkness fell became unsafe, uncomfortable and sometimes impossible. Then the only option was to rely on the chamber pot, which was kept under the bed and pulled out for emergencies. Brenda Haynes of Moulton recalled: 'Pots were kept under the bed and emptied into a pail which we kept under the stairs. This was then taken to the shed when full.' Mrs Haynes remembers how she and her family felt they were 'in clover' when the third bedroom of their house was converted into a modern bathroom in 1933. Mrs Haynes thought she had put the worst behind her, but to her amazement had to use a

Old privy bowls and chamber pots are still serving useful purposes of a more decorative nature.

back yard privy again in 1946 on what was supposed to be the most romantic of occasions, her honeymoon.

A most magnificent chamber pot served Irchester resident Mia Butler's family for many years. It sounds far too grand for its purpose and Mrs Butler still wonders what happened to it. She said: 'It was of basic white, but had raised oval panels at regular intervals, beneath a rim of gold. Each of these oval "medallions" was raised and was of a misty blue shade. The pièce de résistance however, was the delicate subject matter – figures of a sexless angel. Each had a most demure countenance, gowns of intricate folds and vast feathery wings. Each figure was in a slightly different pose, though every face was beatific, pink and glowing. The handle was of gracious curves, the edges in gold relief and the whole pot of enormous capacity. As a child I knew that the appearance and washing of the chamber pot meant that my dad was confined to bed with gout.' Mrs Butler remembers that long after she was married and gone from home the 'angels' used to be put into a large thick brown paper carrier-bag, with reinforced holes for the string handles, and brought to her house when needed.

Mrs Butler also has a friend who uses her ornate chamber pot as home for a goldfish – the only problem being the lack of view for the unfortunate fish.

A rare slipper bed pan can be seen at Wellingborough Heritage Centre. It was found by Judith Thompson in an old barn at her home at Old Farm in Wilby. The white pan bears the inscription 'This Slipper should be passed under the Patient in front between the legs. If a flannel cap is made for the back, fastened

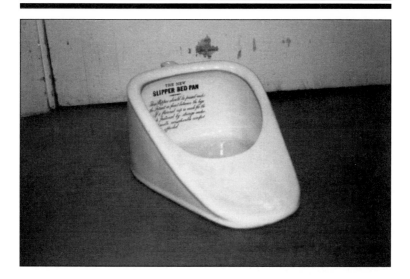

This slipper pan was discovered in an old barn in Wilby. It now sits in Wellingborough Heritage Centre.

by strings under the handle, considerable comfort will be afforded'. Incidentally, there used to be two privies next to the duck house at Old Farm, but they were removed in 1954.

[9]

PUBLIC INCONVENIENCES

This book has so far mainly concentrated on privies at home, but sanitary arrangements obviously had to be made in workplaces and public buildings too.

Along with Victorian schools came wooden desks, blackboards, caning and of course, outside loos. Whilst most managed separate cubicles and drainage facilities, this wasn't always the case. The primary school in Shelley Street, Northampton, is remembered vividly for its insanitary conditions in the late 1930s by 93-year-old Leslie Atkins who was in charge of sewers and waste disposal in the town at the time. 'I had to inspect their arrangements and was amazed that the toilets were not separate. A channel pipe used to go along the length of the building and the sewage flopped into this channel and flushed away. I was responsible for getting them altered.' Mr Atkins remembers that this system was very draughty for the children, as well as unpleasant.

Older people in Irthlingborough still have vivid memories of the now demolished fearful loos at the infants' school. Hilda Britten of Highfield Road attended the school during the 1920s. 'There was a row of six toilets and they were horrible. We used to hang on and hang on and only go when we absolutely had to.' Stan Houghton of Station Road started at the school in 1916. He said: 'They were filthy. There were no flushes and the caretaker had to flush them through, but with all those kids you can imagine how distasteful it became.'

If you thought that outside lavatories at schools in Northamptonshire were now just a distant memory, you would be wrong. At Irchester Infants' School the youngest and oldest children

77

The outside lavatory block at Irchester Infants' School, still used by five and six year olds.

enjoy all mod cons, but the year 1 children, aged five to six, still have to skip from their separate Victorian classrooms to the brick-built lavatories outside. In summer the pupils generally enjoy the excuse to nip outside in the fresh air, but on wet and windy winter days it's a different matter. My own two children attended the school and although my little boy was not bothered by the dash outdoors, my daughter Emma was most upset. She hated the cold, dark and dreary lavatory block and was scared when rain struck against the corrugated iron roof, making quite a clatter.

Northamptonshire is well known for its footwear industry, and before the Second World War a huge number of people were employed either in shoe or boot factories or in a related industry such as tanneries. Back in the early part of the century, factories would commonly have a row of lavatories in a line with a central drain which would run underneath all the cubicles. In the biggest factories, this drain would flow from floor to floor down to the sewers. Buildings historian Brian Giddings of Towcester tells of a common prank which would cause some lighthearted relief for the men and women who spent long hours at tedious work. 'The workers would get an oily rag, set light to it and drop it at the top end of the drain. They would then stand back and hear all the yells as it went down a row of lavatories.'

A Northampton pensioner who worked as a building site fore-man in the 1920s described one of the first jobs when starting work on a new site. Apparently someone was given the task of digging a six foot trench and a pole was balanced across it. Anyone wanting to relieve themselves would have to manage

A 1950s picture of a Northampton building site. Earlier, during the 1920s, workmen would dig a trench and balance a pole across it as a makeshift privy.

on this precarious make-do privy, often with unfortunate consequences.

An alternative trick for unbashful Northampton street workers was to remove the manhole covers in the middle of roads and put their own makeshift toilet arrangement over the top. The introduction of temporary 'tents' for workmen would have come as a great relief to those not keen on doing their business in the middle of the street. More than a decade later in 1937 building site workers were still balancing on poles over holes according to Reg Baldwin of Kingsthorpe. He remembers accidents too, particularly a chap in a smart blue suit who had a messy topple backwards. Mr Baldwin also remembers men having to throw shovelfuls of lime into the hole after use.

DOWN IN THE DEPTHS . . .

Leslie Atkins probably knows more about Northampton's old sewerage system than anyone else and he remembers many aspects of his work very clearly. He believes he was given his job with the former Northampton Corporation partially because of a tragedy which occurred in the town's sewers in 1937. It seems that two men died at Countess Road when chemicals used in the tanning process flowed into the sewerage system and caused poisonous gases. The disaster meant new health and safety policies had to be put into practice quickly, to avoid any similar tragedy.

Although sewers were then in place in Northampton, not everyone was fortunate enough to be linked up to the system. Mr Atkins said: 'One of the first jobs plonked on my desk was to make sure the soil buckets in the Dallington area were emptied. I had to organise a man, Mr Waite, to go round at night to empty all these things. I also had to organise for the cesspits to be emptied, and there were a lot of them in Northampton at that time.'

One of the first jobs assigned to me as a keen fledgling reporter was to don a yellow waterproof, overalls and welly boots and take a trip down into Northampton's underground sewerage system. This entailed trudging round in semi-darkness through ankle deep sludge, trying to avoid breathing too deeply because of the disgusting pong. The purpose of this delightful exercise is long since forgotten, but I do remember the deep admiration I felt for those workers who had to paddle around in the sewers every day. For many years Mr Atkins was one of those who would habitually go underground to determine what to do when things went wrong. He recalls: 'I have crawled about in a lot of the sewers, most of which are egg shaped and about three feet high by two feet wide. It was a far from pleasant job.' There were dangers too, and in the early days Mr Atkins would take along oxygen apparatus and resuscitation equipment when he ventured underground. 'When I first started we had to use tallow candles, we would knock bricks out of the walls and put the candles in. It was nothing to be met by two or three rats whilst crawling along.' Mr Atkins says he has no fear of rats and has grabbed hold of them several times, but fortunately none ever bit him.

On one occasion Mr Atkins decided to have a blitz on rats and had two gangs of two men working on the job for some time. The workers would place a tray of rusks in the brickwork within sight of manholes. They would return the next day and see if anything had been eaten, if so they would put down a lethal cocktail of bread mashed with poison. The dead rats all started washing up at the local sewerage farm – hundreds every day.

Mr Atkins tells of one particular incident when he was called out to a dentist's house in Wellingborough Road one Saturday evening following heavy rain. The dentist was having a big party and had unwisely put all the delicacies for his guests in the basement. Unfortunately, the sewer had become blocked and the basement became flooded, leaving some rather unappetising food and some very hungry guests.

[1 0]

POSH LOOS

Surviving privies are generally to be found amidst cobwebs, flaking paint and the odd mouse's nest. Not so the one at Boughton House near Kettering, which has to be the county's most sumptuous lavatory. The 'thunderbox' is located in a large bathroom adjoining the principal guest room and over the years has been used by many distinguished visitors including members of the royal family and Winston Churchill. The room also doubles up as a ladies' powder room when large functions are held and the sight of the water closet usually causes great surprise and amusement.

Boughton House is the home of the Duke of Buccleuch and Queensbury and was originally a monastic building dating from the mid 15th century. Surprisingly, this magnificent house was closed up and unlived in for more than 100 years until the present duke's mother started major renovation work in the early part of the 20th century. It is believed that the mahogany water closet was probably installed during this restoration process in 1907 when the plumbing and heating work was carried out. The bathroom is completely dominated by two Mortlake tapestries depicting the life of a Roman emperor, and also contains a fireplace and oil painting. Boughton House is open to the public in August, but unfortunately the impressive first floor bathroom is out of bounds. It can, however, be viewed by appointment.

Top prize for the most ornate lavatory goes to the Victorian porcelain model at the Theatre Guild in Claire Street,

Fit for a king – the 'thunderbox' in the principal guest bathroom at Boughton House near Kettering. The drawer contains paper and the system is flushed by pulling a small handle.

This beautifully decorated lavatory is at the Theatre Guild in Claire Street, Northampton.

Northampton. The Invictas washdown closet is beautifully decorated with red and gold flowers, fringed with plenty of deep green foliage. Unfortunately this little gem is spoiled by the black plastic seat and its dingy surroundings including worn green nylon carpet.

Three original and rather splendid Victorian lavatories are still in use at the Guildhall in Northampton. The imposing town centre building opened in 1864, but was refitted in 1892 and it is likely that the lavatories date from then. When they were first installed, more than a century ago, the lavatories must have caused quite a sensation, bearing in mind the more primitive amenities to which most people were used. Town hall keeper John Dunkley said: 'They must have been quite a novelty at the

One of the three original Victorian lavatories still in use at the Guildhall, Northampton.

86

Section of "WAVELET" CLOSET.

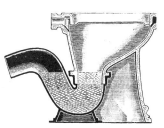

"WAVELET" CLOSET, with
Plain Surface.

The Lead Trap is made with large Socket
for Cement Joint.

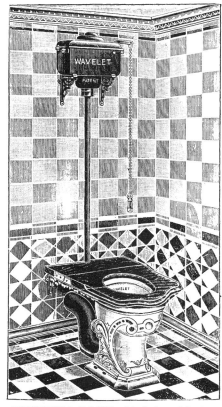

"WAVELET" CLOSET, with Embossed Surface.

With 4in. Lead Trap that can be turned in any direction and soldered to Lead Soil Pipe, ensuring a perfecty sound joint.

	With "P" Trap. each.	With "S" Trap. each.
White Earthenware "Wavelet" Closet, with Embossed Surface... No. 01415	£2 5 6	No. 01417 £2 8 6
White Earthenware "Wavelet" Closet, with Plain Surface ... No. 01416	£2 5 6	No. 01418 £2 8 6

Two Gallon Painted Cast-iron "**Wavelet**" Pull-and-Let-Go Cistern and Cover with Brackets, Chain and Pull ... 20/–
1¼in. Polished Mahogany Seat, with Side Brass Hinges 14/6
1¼in. „ „ with Brass Side Hinges, and Hinged Cover 26/–
Pair of Cast Iron Seat Brackets 5/6

EXTRAS.—If with Two-Gallon "**Smithfield**" Syphon Cistern, instead of the "**Wavelet**" Cistern ... 22/6
If with extra strong Lead Trap with **Porcelain lining** 8/–

138

From the price list of A. Bell & Co Ltd of Northampton dated 1920-1926.

time and I suppose to have the latest flush technology was an extravagance.' The first model was for jurors, adjacent to the room where they retired to deliberate their verdicts. The jurors would have been able to sit on a decorative Deluge model and contemplate the fate of the accused in some comfort.

Another lavatory was originally intended for the magistrate, now used for the council leader, and is a little grander, probably on account of his prestigious position. There is an unusual small china washbasin to the side which tops up with a counterbalance so it cannot flood. The wooden seat is beautifully carved, the white base is a masterpiece and even the patented enamel puller is ornate.

There is a third antique lavatory in the west end basement, originally used by staff and jurors. A formidable enamel sign nearby says 'No rags or sticks to be pushed beneath this water closet'. Mr Dunkley pointed out that even the sewers beneath were something special: 'They are lined with glazed bricks which seems very elaborate for a public building. It seems that the Victorians put a high priority on the job.'

[11]

SERVICEMEN'S TALES

If you thought things were bad for Northamptonshire people before the advent of the modern day lavatory, spare a thought for the local lads who were sent overseas. Even today, sanitary conditions in some countries leave a lot to be desired, but troops often found themselves in foreign climes with no provision whatsoever. It was up to them to use a little ingenuity to create their own privy as best they could. One ex-army man from Irchester told me how he would find a tree and dig a pit near it, then climb up to a handy branch and use it as a seat.

George Kitchen, aged 73, who lives in Tennyson Road, Rushden, has a fascinating story which he swears is true, about his time serving in North Africa with infantry in early 1943. Mr Kitchen later became a prisoner of war but was able to return to the county to work as a shoemaker. He said: 'I was detailed by the CSM to build a latrine for the lads. I tried to explain to the officer that it would be very difficult owing to the lack of material. I was told abruptly that it was up to me to use my initiative.

'Looking around I discovered a large wooden cart wheel half buried in the sand. I then proceeded to dig a large deep hole in the sand and I then placed the cart wheel over the top of the hole, supported at each corner by four large biscuit tins. When it was in use we all sat back to back in a circle. The crowning glory was a palm tree erected in the centre where the axle had been, so that we all sat in the shade.

'A few days later we were pushed back temporarily. The

Germans were fascinated by my invention, and being a bit slow on the uptake, it was some time before they discovered what it was. One German officer, more intelligent than the others, said that it was a diabolical British weapon. But once they found out what it was, it became very popular with the Hermann Goering Panzer division and it wasn't long before they were queuing up to get on it.

'I learned later from a Jerry prisoner that Field Marshal Rommel had used my latrine. In fact, they had a job to get him off it. It was here that he planned his strategy.

'I heard later that it was in constant use until Tunisia fell. Then some idiot threw a fag end into it and the whole thing blew up.'

Andrew Clare of Far Cotton, Northampton, spent 25 years in HM Forces, so knows a thing or two about sanitary conditions overseas. He recalls his time with the 2nd Battalion (Lincolnshire, Leicestershire and Northamptonshire) of the Royal Anglian Regiment on exercise in Kenya: 'Due to the heat and so on the platoon latrines in the "field" always ponged a little after a day's use, so the Quartermaster at the time decided he would have his own personal one built. The ground was like concrete and explosives had to be used to dig the hole.

'One soldier got caught using the QM's loo and was given five extra guard duties for his troubles. Since the lad helped build the loo, we his platoon buddies thought he had been severely and unfairly punished and decided to get some payback. The seat was made from two logs, high and low, on "Y" forks. Since the QM was regular as clockwork the whole platoon used the QM's loo and only lightly sprinkled the outcome with soil prior to his visit. When everyone had finished we rigged the seat to collapse as soon as weight was applied. He didn't come up smelling of roses – and no more personal loos were built.'

George Freeston of Blisworth has clear memories of an airfield in wartime where the communal privy was a wonderfully friendly place: 'It was 25ft long and quite deep. All one had to sit on was a scaffold pole, lodged precariously as there was nothing to hold on to. It was fearsome to sit on, we were like birds perched on a branch of a tree.

'One fellow had such an enormous dropping that it stood up instead of collapsing and friends came from all over the airfield to see what this man had done. They were so impressed that they put a red bow on it.'

[1 2]

BURIED BUT NOT FORGOTTEN

Here's an interesting thought to finish with. If you happen to live in a home in Northamptonshire built more than 50 years ago, there's a good chance that something deeply unpleasant lies buried out there in the garden. Now you know why your runner beans do so well...

———————————

AND FINALLY . . .

This rhyme was published in the *Northampton Chronicle* around 1930:

It is my firm belief
That feeding through the leaf
Will make all crops as healthy as can be;
And after careful test,
I find urine is the best –
It feeds the plants and keeps them insect-free.

All plants do truly need
A much-diluted feed;
And this is how dilution should be done –
To eight pints of water
Add urine one quarter;
In other words, just thirty-two to one.

Sprayed gently on the leaf,
Above and underneath.
It kills the pests and checks the mildew, too.
The growth it seems to charm,
And flowers take no harm
Sprayed once a week with one in thirty-two.

A Privy by Any Other Name

The word 'privy' is an early Middle English word which derives from the Latin 'privatus' meaning secret or apart. Many families in the county had their own special names for privies. Words and phrases associated with the WC are also included.

A 'certain' place
Adam and Eve
Asterroom
Biffy
Bog
Boghouse
Bombay
Chain of Events
Chamberlain pianos ('bucket lav')
Chamber of Commerce
Chuggie
Closet
Comfort station
Crapper box
Crapphouse
Crapping castle
Crapping kennel
Dike
Dinkum-dunnies
Doneks
Dunnekin
Dunnick

Dyke
Flushes and Blushes
Garden loo
Garde robe
Go and have a Jimmy Riddle
Go and have a Tim Tit
Going to inspect the plumbing
Going to pick the daisies
Going to see a man about a dog
Going to spend a penny
Going to stack the tools
Going to the George
Going to the groves
Going where the wind is always blowing
Gong
Gong house
Heads
Here is are
Holy of holies
Honk

House of commons
House of office
Knickies
Larties
Latrine
Lav
Lavatory
Little House
Loo
Nessy
Netty
Out the back
Petty
Place of easement
Place of repose
Place of retirement
Reading room
Round-the-back
Shit hole
Shitush
Shooting gallery
Shunkie
Slash house
The backhouse
The boggy at the
  bottom
The bush
The dispensary
The dunny
The grot
The halting station Hoojy-boo
  (attributed to Dame Edith
  Evans)

The house where the emperor
  goes on foot
The hum
The jakers
The jampot
The japping
The John
The lats
The long drop
The opportunity
The ping-pong house
The plumbing
The porcelain pony
The proverbial
The Sammy
The shants
The shot-tower
The sociable
The tandem (a two holer)
The thinking house
The throne room
The water box
The watteries
The wee house
The whajucallit
Three-(and more) seater
Thunderbox
Two seater
Urinal
Waterloo
Widdlehouse
Windsor Castle
'Yer Tiz'

ACKNOWLEDGEMENTS

Grateful thanks to:
The *Northampton Chronicle & Echo*,
Northampton Abington Park Museum and
Saint Peter's Historical Group, Irthlingborough.